Outsourcing Redefined

Leveraging Remote/Virtual Teams

J. W. Oliver Jr.

Outsourcing Redefined

Indpendently Published

Copyright © 2023, J. W. Oliver Jr.

Published in the United States of America

230330-02283.2

ISBN: 9798392692538

Here's What's Inside…

Introduction
Redefining Outsourcing

The Why and the What of Insourcing

Outsourcing refers to the practice of hiring an external company or individual to perform tasks or services that would otherwise be performed by in-house staff. This could include tasks such as customer service, accounting, or software development. Outsourcing can be done domestically within the same country or internationally, and it can be done onshore (within the same country) or offshore (in a different country). Offshoring specifically refers to the practice of outsourcing tasks or services to a foreign country, typically one where labor costs are lower. This could include outsourcing call center operations to various countries. Many will refer to this as "Remote/Virtual" teams and can include onshore, offshore, and near shore.

Insourcing is truly "outsourcing redefined". This concept was born with the idea of utilizing remote/virtual teams who become part of your culture, your team, and your mission. There are some essential steps to ensuring you have a healthy culture that integrates your in-office teams with your Insourced teams:

- Establish a clear communication strategy: Ensure that remote and virtual team members have access to the necessary communication tools and protocols, such as email, instant messaging, video conferencing, and project management software. Encourage regular check-ins and establish guidelines for response times and availability.

- Foster a sense of inclusion: Include remote and virtual team members in company-wide initiatives, such as company events, team-building exercises, and training sessions. Consider setting up a virtual water cooler, where team members can chat and socialize outside of work-related conversations.

- Set expectations for work output and performance: Clearly communicate goals, objectives, and expectations for remote and virtual team members. Ensure that they understand how their work fits into the larger picture and provide regular feedback on their performance.

- Establish a consistent onboarding process: Ensure that remote and virtual team members receive the same level of onboarding and training as on-site employees. Provide them with the necessary tools and resources to do their jobs effectively.

- Encourage cross-functional collaboration: Encourage remote and virtual team members to collaborate with on-site employees and foster a culture of knowledge-sharing and idea generation. This can be facilitated through regular team meetings, brainstorming sessions, and cross-functional projects.

- Create opportunities for career development: Offer remote and virtual team members the same opportunities for career development and advancement as on-site employees. Provide them with access to training, mentorship, and professional development programs.

- SWAG! Everyone loves good swag. Send your teams t-shirts, pens, koozies, etc.

By implementing these methods, you can help integrate remote and virtual teams into your office culture and foster a more collaborative and inclusive work environment. You now have fostered happier and healthier teams and long-term committed members of your business.

For the past few decades, there has been a trend of skepticism toward "outsourcing". There were issues such as:

- Language and accent barriers
- Time zones
- Culture variances
- Technology to communicate.

Companies like ZimWorX have developed a new path to ensure these issues are mitigated or solved and actually turn remote/virtual teams into a more productive, efficient, and satisfying environment for a business to grow. This has proven to be an effective plan for a business to thrive through good and difficult economic times.

J. W. Oliver Jr.

Chapter One
The Big Problem with Hiring

Number One Complaint

The number one complaint we hear from businesses worldwide is the cost of bringing on new employees. It's just so expensive. First are the hard costs of salary and benefits: health insurance, dental insurance, payroll taxes, 401(k), and more. Then there are the costs of providing a productive work environment: a desk, a computer, heat and air conditioning, electricity, office chairs, filing cabinets, and lighting. Then, what if you also need to rent or purchase more office space to house your new employees? You will need to remodel the space to your needs, purchase more office furniture, pay even higher utility bills, and so on. Before you know it, you will likely spend $4,000 to $5,000 upfront for every new person you hire. Yikes!

It doesn't end there. Once the shock wears off, the realization of the hidden cost of time for you or your H.R. department to complete the entire hiring process from start to finish will come into play. (Heaven forbid you to need to hire a recruiting firm to assist you... Cha-ching!)

As business owners sit down and calculate all of these costs upfront, they often become discouraged, especially if they come up a bit short on funds. As a result, companies don't expand or grow in certain areas because they just can't afford it. Everyone knows, if you are not growing, you are stagnating and possibly even regressing, but it's not only businesses that suffer. Entrepreneurs are negatively affected as well. Often, great ideas are thwarted before the dream ever gets off the ground because entrepreneurs look at all the costs and determine they can't take the risk. There is just no way they can absorb all the employee costs for three, six, or even nine months as they begin their launch into greatness.

What If?

Most companies, large or small, operate within a limited profit range. When they begin to look at hiring new employees to delve into a new sector or initiative, the allocation of the necessary resources may move them from being a profitable company to an unprofitable one. In the short term, this is something most can't afford to do.

What if there were a less expensive alternative? What if a company could cut the costs of bringing on a new employee by as much as fifty percent? How about seventy-five percent? What if you could get an employee for $24,000 who would typically cost you $60,000? What if you could get an employee for $40,000 who would usually cost you $110,000? What if the lower-cost employee were equally as qualified? That could potentially change everything!

ZimWorX Can Make It Happen.

Over the years, our team at ZimWorX has created a scalable system to reduce the costs mentioned above and save companies substantial amounts of money. This unique program will dramatically decrease your payroll by reducing salaries AND eliminating hard and soft costs. Through this system, you will be able to grow your company and take on new challenges. How? By utilizing the highly qualified team members found within our Insourcing program.

Chapter Two
Outsourcing Redefined "Insourcing"

What Is Insourcing?

Insourcing is a process that allows you to bring on full-time, remote-working employees who work for you, no one else. Once hired, they are turned over to you to train and manage. Through the miracle of technology, these employees fully integrate within your team and become valuable members of your staff. They work the same hours, attend the same meetings, work on the same projects as your in-house staff, and have the same education. The only difference is that they are not physically in your office space or building, but with the fast connectivity of technology today, they might as well be.

Remote Working Becomes Real

As a result of the COVID-19 pandemic, many companies decided to allow their employees to work from home. After all, they still needed to have their scheduling, accounting, marketing, websites, customer care, and other necessities continue. During that process, many discovered that remote workers perform quite well and offer a variety of cost savings. Even with this knowledge, the question remained: "Should we, as a company, really consider moving toward remote workers as a future strategy?"

Key to Moving Forward? A New Mindset

It's important to note that, as you think about bringing on remote employees to your team, you need to develop a new mindset. If you're at all like me, you're probably a control freak. I say this because, in the past, I needed to know what everybody was doing all the time. I wanted my employees to be close to me, so I could walk by their desks and see if they were doing what they were supposed to be doing. However, the anxiety and stress of keeping up with everyone were driving me crazy. Eventually, I realized I had control issues. Over time, I began to change my mindset. As an employer, I realized I should be focused on the productivity levels of my employees, not what they were doing every moment of the day.

I began to ask myself, "Are they completing their tasks? Are they meeting the standards in demand? Are they often going above and beyond what I ask?" If they were, in the end, that was all that truly mattered. I didn't need to micromanage after all. Once I had adopted this mindset, it didn't matter if my employees were in my office or in another country. All that mattered was the work getting done. I became happier and healthier, my employees became happy and healthier, and my business began to grow. With this new mindset, I was now primed and ready to succeed in the new reality of remote working.

The Takeaway

Insourced employees are of great value and can produce results equal to on-site staff. However, this realization requires a change in how businesses look at their employees. They need to recognize that having everyone under the same roof is unnecessary while also understanding that remote working through Insourcing is a viable and necessary alternative for the future.

Chapter Three

The Difference Between Freelancers and Insourcing

What Is Freelancing?

At this point, you may be asking yourself what the difference is between Insourcing and freelance workers. Typically, people who freelance and outsource their work, whether in the United States or out of the country, spend their energy with several clients at the same time. Because of this, the freelancer will usually acquire and perform several projects simultaneously. If their schedule fills up, they won't be able to work on your project, which means you need to look for someone else. Also, since most freelance outsourcing work is project-based, your costs will vary wildly depending on several factors.

How busy is the freelancer? If they are in high demand, they will charge more. How qualified is the freelancer? Skill levels vary greatly. The more gifted they are, the more you will pay.

Overseas Freelancing Difficulties

If you decide to outsource a freelancer overseas, you will often need to overcome language and culture barriers. Will the freelancer be able to adequately understand your project so that they will be able to complete it correctly with minimal effort on your part? Will the freelancer be able to produce a product that coincides with the cultural nuances of Western society? If the freelancer needs to interact with clients or customers, will they be able to be understood? If not, this will be a frustrating and challenging process for you. Without adequate communication and cultural familiarity, businesses will find themselves going back to the freelancer several times to get a project right. Doing so increases the stress on you, wastes time, and causes productivity to fall.

Are the Needed Tools Available?

Beyond the workload, culture, and language, another obstacle to overcome is the freelancer's tools and workspace. Whenever you use outsourced or freelance personnel, you have to rely on their infrastructure and equipment.

Do they have a good internet connection for communicating, downloading, and uploading? Do they take proper security measures to make sure your content is safe? How do they back up their data? Will they have electricity only at certain times of the day? Do they have a space with an environment that is conducive to work and free of noise and distraction? If your freelancer is ill-equipped to handle all aspects of your job, your frustration will only grow as the project moves forward.

We currently work with a medical imaging company that used to have 12 freelancers based in five different locations around the world. They joined us because of the continuous infrastructure and connection issues on the freelancers' side, which significantly inhibited communication during their essential group meetings.

Will They Be Loyal?

If you find the right freelancer who does excellent work for you, you will quickly discover a desire to keep them. Unfortunately, their loyalty to you and your projects often depends on what you can pay. A friend told me over 20 years ago, "You'll have the most loyal person working for you until somebody offers him 25 cents more an hour. He'll then drop you like a hot potato." That is always a risk.

Barking Dogs and Roosters

The time difference between freelancers and businesses can also be challenging. For many years, one of the individuals who had worked for me the longest was in India. She was on the phone every day, interacting with my customers. Problems arose because of the time difference between her and my customers. She would start early in the morning while her husband was sleeping and begin making her calls. Every day, like clockwork, several roosters would begin to crow midway through her work hours. Then, on cue, all the dogs in the neighborhood would start to bark. It was quite comical for my customers, who were working late in the afternoon, to hear an early morning wake-up call from nature on the other side of the world. However, as you can imagine, that wasn't the most professional representation of my company (even though I look back now and smile).

How Is Insourcing with Us Different from Working with a Freelancer?

Insourced Employees Work Only for You.

Our team members are full-time employees who work solely for you. The only projects they will have to juggle are the ones that you give to them.

With Us, English Is the First Language, and Our Culture is Western

With our company, your team member speaks "Queen's English" as their first language, with a British accent. Their culture is also heavily influenced by Western thought as a result of being a British colony for many years.

Great Working Conditions Are a Given.

Our offices are housed on the ninth floor of a beautiful high-rise building in downtown Harare. Your team member will have a workspace with the latest computers, with all the necessary security and infrastructure in place, keeping their work product and your data safe. We can even provide a conference room to gather all of your team member together in one space for your team meetings. We have found that the excellence of our office space fosters a level of professionalism in your Team member employee that your clients can distinguish.

Our People Have a Special Sense of Loyalty

Our team members genuinely want to come to work. While many of our teams live in urban suburbs around the city, they're able to come into a beautiful office facility where they are proud to work. We strive to be the envy of every company in our industry by attracting top talent. Our employees are paid above-average wages and in American dollars, something that only a few companies in the country do.

Our class A working conditions often keep them from "jumping ship" after having trained them to a high level. In our offices, they enjoy A/C in the hot summer months, upscale workrooms, cheerful workspaces, and even a cafeteria. Best of all, the team members form a great camaraderie with those around them. It's a young group. The average age of the team members in our office is 28 years old. Therefore, you have a young, energetic group wanting to learn, grow, and develop their skill sets. These factors keep our team members loyal and make us a very desirable place to be employed and stay employed.

We Provide Strong Security for Your Data

Data security is critical to us. The danger of outsourcing is that those doing your work may be working from their home or remote office. If so, they might not have the data security systems necessary to protect you. We, however, use the highest-rated secure routers, which are programmed to be up to date with all the current annual licenses and software.

On our computers, we deactivate the USB ports so no external storage devices can be connected. As a further precaution, we can also limit access to specific sites as requested by the client. For example, suppose you want your employee not to have access to particular information or URLs. In this case, we will program their computer to access only your approved sites from their workstation.

Concerning storage and connectivity, we utilize a primary server and two redundant servers as backups. For connectivity, we use a robust fiber-optic network with latency, very similar to what you would find when you connect with a company in the USA.

We Go Above and Beyond

In terms of on-site support for your remote workers, we have a general manager, an I.T. team, client liaisons, and a full H.R. department. To top it all off, we provide two full-time employees in our pastoral care. These are trained pastors who assist your team members in times of need. Our pastors attend family funerals and help your employees by counseling them on matters such as divorce or financial difficulties. They are also there to help your employee when making big life decisions. We're one of only two companies I know of that provide this, and we do it free of charge.

A Client Story

One of our clients works for a large healthcare coaching firm in the Northwest that chose us because of what we offered. As part of their company culture, they always include their two remote workers in their fifteen-minute, stand-up morning huddles. Here, they bring in everyone to talk about what they'll be working on throughout the day. Because the client's remote workers are Insourced, they easily fit into that meeting and feel a part of the overall team. Also, since the remote workers are full-time, constant members of the team, this client always knows whom to ask about a particular issue or question.

The Takeaway

The utilization of remote workers is fast becoming the norm in businesses today. When you decide to go in that direction, there are many options to choose from in finding the right employee to work remotely for you. Freelance outsourcing can be useful for one-off projects such as brochures, language translation, or a quick website. However, if you are looking for a sustained, full-time workforce with all the tools needed to succeed and make your business grow, we believe Insourcing is the only way to go.

We equip team members with top-of-the-line equipment and reliable internet for seamless communication.

The conference room allows teams to gather for group meetings.

Team members utilize private workstations.

The ZimWorX office is located on the ninth floor of the prestigious Joina City building in downtown Harare.

Working with mothers of disabled children is an example of how Global Impact is making a difference.

Global Impact distributed food packages that helped 322 families during the pandemic.

Our leadership team gets excited to do ministry!

Beautiful Africa

It's truly a blessing to work with the people of Zimbabwe and make an impact.

Chapter Four
Zimbabwe: The People

Is the Education Level in Zimbabwe Comparable to The United States?

When I first started this venture three years ago, I was concerned about the level of education in Zimbabwe. My thought process was telling me, "I'm going to have to sift through a bunch of paperwork to find somebody who's up to my standards." However, I quickly found out that, of the 54 countries in Africa, Zimbabwe ranks first or second in education level every year. The reason for this is that Zimbabwe follows a British-based education system that gets results.

In addition to this, families place a high emphasis on their children's education. Parents will go through extreme measures and gather their resources to ensure a university degree is within reach of their child. A degree, by the way, which is on par with the United States. Parents do this for one reason. A solid education is considered the best way for their child to find a better life in their underperforming economy.

Will I Be Able to Understand My Employee?

Zimbabwe is a former British colony, where English is the people's first language, not a "picked-up" second language. Their accent is authentically British and easy to understand. Before I first started ZimWorX, I was using contracted workers through Upwork and various other outsourcing modules for my dental imaging and equipment company. However, using them was a constant struggle as language was always an issue. When I came upon this particular opportunity in Zimbabwe with my partner, who was born there, I discovered a group of people who speak the Queen's English! I find joy in interacting with them regularly. Zimbabweans speak such excellent English, and many of our clients utilize them to contact their customers on the phone.

What Kinds of Skills Will I Be Able to Find in Zimbabwe?

There has yet to be a case where we could not find an employee to fill a client's needs. When you start looking, the key is to think outside of the box and dream about positions you wish you could fill. Should I hire someone to relieve the stress of my overworked staff? How about a new position that might jump-start my business's creativity? What about hiring someone skilled in advertising to get my product known in my community? These are questions every growing business should be asking itself.

As you ask yourself those questions, here are a few of the many skills we can find to take your business to new heights:

- Accounts Receivable Director

- Customer Service Specialist

- Data Entry Manager
- Back End/Front End Web Developer
- Insurance Verification/Call Backs/Patient Follow-up
- Personal Assistant
- Accounts Manager
- Financial Analyst
- I.T. Consultant
- Systems Analyst
- Distribution Manager
- App Developer
- Content Writer
- Social Media Specialist
- Art Development
- 2D and 3D Animator
- Video and Sound Specialist
- Sales Assistant

These are just the tip of the iceberg. No matter the position, we will work hard to find what you need, from lower-level task positions to upper-echelon leaders. If you can dream it and come up with a job description, we will find the right person for you!

What Is Their Working Schedule?

Zimbabwe uses Central African Time (CAT) which is between six and nine hours ahead of the continental United States, depending on the client's time zone. However, the time zone differences do not need to be considered when setting your employee's work hours. Why? Our office is open 24 hours a day, and the team members know that they must sync their schedules with yours. If they need to start their eight-hour shift at 4:00 am or finish work at midnight CAT, they will do it. Typically, the bulk of our team members arrive and work from 3 pm to midnight CAT, which is the typical 8 am to 5 pm shift in Central Time (CST), but there is rarely an hour in the day when someone is not working.

Will My Employee Honor Confidentiality?

All employees sign a non-disclosure agreement (N.D.A.) upon hire. It's important to note that an N.D.A. in Zimbabwe is a highly regarded document. Employees are acutely aware that breaching an N.D.A. goes on their permanent work record, and that is very detrimental to their ability to find future work. Because of this, the people in Zimbabwe, compared to other places, do not share sensitive company information.

Do They Desire to Work?

In Zimbabwe, the unemployment rate is over 80%, yet it is a country with more than 2 million university-educated employees. Jobs that are needed to help survive and take care of one's family are scarce. Because of this, people are appreciative of any opportunity to find employment. Also, since we pay good salaries in U.S. currency, we are a sought-after workplace with excellent retention.

What about My Current Employees? Will They Push Back Out of Fear for Their Jobs?

As you begin thinking about using remote workers in Zimbabwe, you may have to deal with some initial fear from your current employees. Your employees will often think, "The practice is going with remote workers now? Oh no! They're going to replace us all!"

You can ease those fears from the beginning by changing your mindset. Help your employees realize that you are hiring remote workers to take care of the many tasks that are currently keeping them from doing their actual jobs. Another perspective would be showing them that you want to add on to grow and expand your business, in which case, everybody wins.

One of our clients faced this from her local employees. After some guidance from us, she cast a vision to her team, showing how this would lighten their workload and enable the company to expand to new areas. She was also able to share that this was an opportunity to give employment to someone who desperately needed it. After hearing this vision, her team got fully on board.

The Takeaway

Zimbabwe is a perfect country to Insource your next employee. As we have seen, the people of Zimbabwe are university educated with degrees on par with the United States. They have qualifications in every area of business. Their first language is English, and they speak the "Queen's English". As a former British colony, they are heavily influenced by Western culture. They desire to work and will work on your schedule. Their society promotes confidentiality. There are very few countries that have remote workers like this.

Chapter Five

Hiring an Employee through Insourcing

Where Do I Begin?

The first step is to let us know what type of employee you are looking to hire. You can do this either by going to our website and filling out the job matrix or by sending us your job description. We will then give you a call to learn more about your company and discover any special requirements we should be aware of when we begin our search.

Once we have found the top three or four candidates, we will set up a Zoom interview according to your schedule. During the interview, you will meet the candidates face to face and speak to them about their qualifications and experience level. This interview usually lasts between thirty and sixty minutes, but you may take as long as you need to ensure you get the right person. Once you find a candidate you want to hire, we will finalize their salary with you and begin the onboarding process. Then, in five to seven days, your new employee will be working for you.

What Do You Provide?

We provide basic workstations with a PC that meets all of the basic specifications for most positions. We also make special provisions for any position that may need to utilize and manipulate large data files, such as animation and graphic design. A few clients have requested higher-level PCs with exact specifications, which we can source locally in Harare. A few have even asked if they could send over their laptops or PCs, which is a request we happily assist with. Once the computers are shipped over, they can then also be maintained by our I.T. team for a small fee.

It's the same with telephone and communication systems. Many of our clients in the medical and insurance industry ship their VoIP phones over to our facility. Once we receive them, we plug that phone into the client's VoIP system, which allows them to contact their employee by simply picking up their phone and dialing an extension. We can also provide a desktop phone extension to plug into the desk modules, which can be bought locally in Zimbabwe. Many of our clients also communicate solely through new systems such as RingCentral™, Zoom, and WhatsApp.

Also, for security and connectivity, we provide redundancies on our fiber internet connections, should an unforeseen problem occur with one of our providers.

What Will This Cost Me, and How Can I Pay?

Once you hire your employee, you will pay a one-time onboarding fee of 50% of their salary to get them started. From then on, you will be billed a flat-rate monthly fee. Since your new employee is considered a contract employee, your monthly payment is paid directly to us.

This gives you the added savings of no payroll taxes or insurance costs. As far as the actual payment process is concerned, you can pay via A.C.H. direct bank wire, check, or credit card.

How Many Employees Am I Required to Hire?

Often, outsourcing companies that offer services similar to ours require a minimum of five to ten team members to begin. Then, as you grow, you are up-charged as you scale from there. With us, there is no upper or lower limit to the number of employees you can hire, and there is no upcharge as you add more. You can choose to hire one, or you can hire two hundred and still pay the same per employee.

How Long Can an Employee Work for Me?

We provide all our clients with a 30-day service agreement. From that point on, everything is on a 30-day rolling, auto-renewing service agreement. You can hire someone for one month, or you can have them for the next twenty years.

How Do You Vet Your Prospects?

We go through all applicable resumes to see who has the best-matching skill sets. Once those candidates are selected, we initiate a preliminary, internal interview with our H.R. department. This allows us to determine how the candidates present themselves, how well they communicate, and how well they know their subject matter. Once this is complete, we then run a criminal background check on the candidates who pass this first round. If everything comes back clear, we will set up a Zoom interview between them and you. If the candidate meets your needs, you can then hire them. If not, we will keep looking for you until we find someone who does.

Are There Any Taxes and Paperwork Involved?

With us, you are contracting a "leased employee" through our Texas-based L.L.C. Because of this, there are no taxes involved. Beyond the initial signed agreement, all you have to do is send us a 1099 form for your employee's wages. You don't have to fill out I-9s, W-2s, W-3s, or W-4s over the course of the year. It's painless.

We Do the Work with No Obligation.

We understand that your time is valuable, so we work hard to get a new team member for you quickly and easily. We will search for an employee, vet them, set up an interview, and then do all the onboarding to get them set up to begin working for you. The best part of all of this? The up-front work doesn't cost you a penny. No agreements are signed until you are ready to hire your new team member.

In essence, we do all the legwork to find you a great employee for free. Why? We firmly believe that nine times out of ten, we will locate an employee who is perfect for you, and when we do, you will hire them. The key is to move forward and just get started. If it's not right for you, there's no obligation. You give us your requirements, go through the process, do the video interview, and see what happens. If you are not pleased, you can walk away without paying a thing.

What do you have to lose?

Key Takeaway

Finding and hiring a new employee doesn't have to be an arduous process. Send us your requirements, and we will take care of everything for you. You can then focus on the things in your business that need your attention.

Chapter Six
Dental

Director of First Impressions

We don't know where our first impressions come from or precisely what they mean, so we don't always appreciate their fragility. Malcolm Gladwell

What are you doing to make a good first impression when your phone is answered? This isn't a simple answer. Some will say, "Smile, talk slowly, and be interested in the caller," while others will say, "Get to the point and answer their questions," but who is right? They all are! The person answering the phone is the gatekeeper for your business and can make it or break it. Your team member needs to know what type of personality is on the other side of the telephone to create a long-lasting impression. Utilizing a remote team member to answer your phones is essential to the experience that your new clients or patient calls receive. Studies have shown that your caller will decide within the first two minutes of their conversation with your business whether they will accept your recommendations or not.

The Director of First Impressions is someone who can read personality styles, create the trust and confidence your callers need to accept treatment and be detail oriented enough that you are set up for success. Within a business, your phones are constantly ringing, and people are coming and going. Taking this task out of the office allows your in-office team members to focus on the person standing right in front of them and not the one on the phone.

The Director of First Impressions can take ownership of the phone call experience and create a relationship with the client. They can spend as little time or as long as they need to for the caller to feel like you rolled out the red carpet for them. The age of rushing callers is no longer. Many other people can do what you do. It will be about who can do it better.

The best candidate for this position will be someone who has a clear and easy-to-understand phone voice. Previous experience with customer service would be a plus. Oftentimes, that could be retail or hospitality. It is beneficial to find someone who is easy to train and follows directions well, with the ability to learn quickly. You don't want someone in this role who isn't an extrovert because we want relationships to be built in the short time that we have them on the phone.

Lastly, this Director of First Impressions can represent your brand by following up with the caller after their encounter with your business. They can solicit reviews from people with fantastic experiences or possibly hold off a bad review from someone who was left lacking.

Insurance Verification

Insurance verification is a vital step in the Revenue Cycle Management for medical and dental practices. This isn't just a matter of confirming that a patient is eligible for services. It is far greater than that! A successful practice, which is insurance driven, needs to know how much coverage a patient will have for every service that is provided within the office. This requires time, automation, and documentation that many offices don't have the time required to complete properly. It is more important for your in-office team members to provide your patients with an exceptional experience once they walk in the door without having them preoccupied with sitting on hold with an insurance company.

Our team members are trained to not only ask the questions required to complete a verification of benefits that are specifically customized for that practice but they are also trained to enter that information directly into your software your way. "Your systems your way" is our motto and what our team members represent.

Oftentimes, this may take multiple phone calls and fax-back verifications along with online printouts. Leverage a remote team member who can learn exactly how you want your insurance verifications completed and doesn't rely on automation alone.

Surprises are wonderful when they are gifts or visits from friends. Surprise bills to patients are never received with great enthusiasm to immediately send you additional money. These surprise bills can take up more of your team's valuable time explaining and possibly arguing with your valuable patients. It won't matter anymore how you got the patient out of pain or how you were able to work the schedule to get them in at the time they wanted. All they will remember is that you "overcharged them" for the services. If your practice has a comprehensive breakdown of benefits, these calls should be less frequent. You must have transparency in your estimations of benefits from the insurance company so that your patient has a clear expectation of their financial responsibilities.

Lastly, insurance verifications normally are the least liked activity or task within the dental office. Can you imagine sitting on hold with an insurance company for 45 minutes only to have the representative tell you, "I can answer five questions and five questions only," but you have 11 on your list that you need answering? NOT FUN! This can decrease a team member's motivation and the morale of the business team. Now imagine that a team member just completed calling that insurance three times, listening to the same on-hold music, and a new patient is standing in front of them. Will they be able to switch off that irritation mode and roll out the red carpet for that new patient? It takes skill, willpower, and professionalism. There is a way to eliminate the irritations that insurance causes your team, and that is by Leveraging a Remote Team Member.

Revenue Cycle Management

RCM is the equation that leads to the success of your accounting efforts. It is the process by which funds are brought into the office efficiently and effectively. It includes several elements such as knowing the specifics of the insurance plans for your patients, understanding the process of a clean claim, staying on top of your accounts receivable both from patients and insurance, proper communication with your patients regarding the charges, use of technology to assist in your proper collections, and so much more!

Leveraging Remote Team Members for revenue cycle management begins with that first phone call. Your Director of First Impressions has an obligation to the practice and to the patient to gather all the information that will be necessary for obtaining a breakdown of the patient's benefits. Next comes the actual verification with communication to the office on what the patient's coverage offers. Your software should allow for flags, coverage books, payment tables, and even insurance notes so that the communication on benefits is clear.

Next comes the submittal of a clean claim. A clean claim is a submitted claim without any errors or other issues, including incomplete documentation. All attachments, including radiographs, chart notes, periodontal charting, intraoral photos, and even reports from your AI technology, should be attached. If the claim is missing even a birthdate or the relationship between the patient and the subscriber, this will only delay the payment for this claim. Clean claims include but are not limited to the date of service, the member ID number, the birthdate of the subscriber and the patient, any primary and secondary insurance coverage information, as well as the practice information meaning the TIN and the provider license information. When submitting claims, always over-attach and never omit anything. Oftentimes, screenshots of chart notes go a long way to getting a claim paid the first time around.

Collecting payment at the time of service is key. Some offices collect payment in full and allow the assignment of benefits to go directly to the patient, while other offices collect only the estimated patient portion. The word "estimated" is the key ingredient in the last sentence. Highly effective offices communicate to their patients that we are collecting the estimated patient portion based on the information that we receive from their insurance company, but this amount could change after the insurance company has paid on the benefit level they feel is necessary.

Never use the words "CO-PAY" or "Your Out-of-Pocket". The patient will feel that they have already paid everything due without any chance of additional payment being required. It is highly recommended that you also have a credit card on file in such instances that the insurance doesn't pay the amount anticipated on the claim. Be sure to have the patient's prior authorization for any charges and secure the credit card information according to your state's privacy mandates.

When payment is received from the insurance company, it is important to have someone knowledgeable in reading the patient ledgers in your software to determine the correct posting of that claim payment. Payments need to be allocated by the provider, along with any adjustments. Documentation, once again, must explain how the claim was paid, what the insurance company paid, and why. It is recommended that with every claim payment that is posted, there is a note explaining how that payment was applied. An ideal note would look something like this:

> "DOS of 1-1-2023 for JW. The patient was charged $500. Insurance paid $450. Coverage was 50%, but a $50 deductible was applied. The patient owes $550 per Delta Dental of Texas. BJM"

It states what happened and how it affected the account. Another example might look like this:

> "DOS of 1-1-2023 for JW. The patient was charged $500. Insurance paid $300. Delta Dental of Texas combined the radiographs into an FMX as per our contract. PPO fees and this downgrade resulted in an adjustment of $200. The patient owes $0 on this claim as per Delta Dental of Texas. BJM"

Proper posting and proper documentation make it so much easier to track, audit, and explain the account should there ever be a need. You can also see that, if the account balance shows $200, the adjustment wasn't completed per the EOB without having to search for that EOB somewhere in your archives.

Part of the revenue cycle management involves following up on submitted claims. Each insurance company is different in the way they process their claims and how fast they process their claims. One thing is the fact dental offices lose about one billion dollars a year (that is, a Billion with a B) on claims that have to be written off for either untimely filing or submitting dirty claims. Highly efficient offices have a follow-up system in place for claims as soon as they hit 22 working days old. The squeaky wheel gets the oil when it comes to claims processing, and you will need someone to squeak often to get your claims paid quickly.

Patient collections after insurance companies have made their payments are also a part of Revenue Cycle Management. As was previously mentioned, no one likes surprise bills, so be prepared with every single statement that gets sent to defend and explain the balance due. Sending paper statements is a thing of the past, but many offices still do send them. Send them electronically to a clearinghouse for printing and processing. They will be in color, come with a return envelope, and be much more professional than what comes printed from your office.

Since we live in the technology era, many offices have switched to text-to-pay options. Text messages are opened and read almost 138% more than email (98% to 18% open rate), and 90% of all text messages are read within three minutes of being received. Ninety-one percent of Americans keep their mobile devices within arm's length at all times. Many patients report going to their mailbox only after being told to expect something. Do you want to wait for your payments? If not, collect a second form of payment to use if there is a remaining balance or use technology for a click-to-pay option. These are the best methods for ensuring payment from a patient as quickly as possible.

Leveraging remote team members for this task is as easy as finding the right personality to complete the tasks. For this position, it is important to look for someone who is task-driven, organized, and good with numbers, someone who has a bit of a stronger personality to be able to speak to insurance companies, and someone who is going to be a rule follower. The ideal candidate would have some money or accounting background and be able to handle every step of the collections process. We have team members completing every portion of RCM within Support DDS and ZimWorX.

Appointment Confirmation

Automation is everywhere, but what do you do when it fails to provide the desired outcome for your practice? Patient confirmation is one of those areas where practices find automation useful, but you will still have reluctant or non-compliant patients who need to be called. For your office, it is about knowing who will be there and who won't. It is about estimating the production for the day and allocating your team accordingly. However, your patient says, "I scheduled the appointment. Of course, I will be there," or "I didn't get a reminder, so I didn't think I had an appointment."

There are weak words and powerful words that come into play with insurance confirmations. First, when you use the word "JUST", it devalues everything you are about to say, and when you provide options for them to cancel or reschedule, they just may do that. Instead, approach confirmation calls from a customer service aspect. We want to know how we can make the dental experience work for them. It is important to not sound scripted but instead relate to the patient on their level. An example would be something like this:

Team member: *"Hello, Mrs. Jones. This is JW from ABC Dental. Dr. Smith asked me to call you. He wanted to know what questions you might have regarding the one hour he has reserved for you at 3:00 pm on Thursday."*

Patient "None, I'll be there."

Team member: *"That is great news. We will let Dr. Jones know. I want to confirm your email address is ---------, and you can receive text messages at -----------."*

Patient: "Yes."

Team member: *"If you wouldn't mind, could you please bring up the email or the text message and click the box to confirm the appointment? We would like to make* *sure that our system is working properly and that we don't have to bother you with phone calls in the future. We are looking forward to seeing your smile again on Thursday."*

Many times, when you call a patient, you end up leaving a voice message. This is frustrating because they might have a full voicemail, or maybe even the voicemail isn't set up yet. Try a personal text message or a personal email, too. When leaving a voicemail, the following script is recommended.

Team member: *"Hello, Mrs. Jones. This is JW from ABC Dental. Dr. Jones asked me to call you to see what questions you have regarding the one hour he has reserved for you at 3:00 pm on Thursday. If you do not have any questions, please review the email or text message that was sent and kindly click the confirm button so that our office can prepare for your appointment. If you would like to discuss this appointment, please give me a phone call back at (234)-567-9876, and any one of our team members would be happy to speak with you.*

We are looking forward to seeing your smile again on Thursday."

Confirmation of patient appointments is an easy way to get started with a remote team member. You can leverage their personality and allow them to be a valuable resource for your practice by following these guidelines.

Patient Care Follow Up

Do you love your patients? Do you want them to have an over-the-top experience with your practice? You have already heard many excellent ways to Leverage Your Remote Team Members to make that happen. Highly effective practices place patient phone calls for all new patients and anyone who received anesthesia within 24 hours of their appointment. During this call, the goal is to see if their expectations were met and if their overall dental health remains their focus. If compliments are received about the office, a verbal suggestion, followed by an email with the link, to write a review is recommended. If they didn't agree that their care was excellent, a follow-up phone call with your patient concierge would be advised before a bad review is written.

It is also advised that all follow-up calls be documented. This is to protect the office from any allegations or complications that could result from the treatment. Let's say, for instance, a patient received crowns on #8 and #9. During your follow-up call, the patient stated that their crowns looked awesome. Their spouse couldn't believe what a difference it made and how they are smiling all the time now. Document facts: "Patient stated …," not feelings: "Patient was happy." Documenting the facts is important because imagine if the insurance company denied the claim. The patient now owes for the two crowns and starts saying, "I never liked the way they looked. One looks larger than the other, and the color is off." We have documentation that can argue their satisfaction with the services.

Follow-up calls also help your client feel loved, appreciated, and listened to! More often than not, you will receive more compliments than complaints. Here is a sample script to use on a new patient follow-up call:

Team Member: *"Good morning, Mrs. Jones. This is JW with ABC Dental. I am excited to speak with you! I wanted to hear about your visit with Dr. Oliver on Monday. Do you have a couple of minutes to chat?"*

Patient: "Sure. I thought it was great."

Team Member: *"Sounds like it was a successful visit. During our initial phone conversation, you stated that your expectations for us as your new dental home were that our office was clean and we ran on time. Please share with me your thoughts on how we did meet your expectations."*

Patient: "I thought it went pretty well. I mean, I needed more work than I thought I would, but it seemed like the doctor knew his stuff."

Team Member: *"That is good to hear. I do see here that you were given a treatment plan for a couple of visits. Would you like me to have someone go over the treatment with you and answer any additional* *questions that you might have so that you can get started with your dental visits?"*

Patient: "Actually, I am ready to schedule now. Can you help me with that?"

Team Member: *"That is great news. Of course. Let's make an appointment for you. Would you prefer Tuesday at 2:00 pm or Thursday at 10:00 am?"*

Follow-up calls can increase case acceptance, increase the number of internal referrals from your patients, and create lifelong relationships with your patients. These calls do not have to be completed by the doctor or even someone in the office. You can Leverage a Remote Team Member to take on these tasks. This is a perfect opportunity to show your patients that you love and appreciate them.

The Essential Guide to Patient Scheduling, Re-care, and Re-Activation Systems

We all know that we need to have patients on the schedule to keep our dental office afloat. There are different types of patients and different types of appointments. We have all heard that re-care appointments are part of the "bread and butter" of a practice, but what else is? So often, we are trying to fill today's schedule and perhaps tomorrow's, but a challenge is to be proactive and work with our unscheduled patients consistently. You might be very booked in your hygiene schedule, but open to the doctors. You might be challenged in a million different ways, but the bottom line is the more consistently your schedule is booked, the easier it is to take great care of your patients and hit your goals.

There are three main ways that you should schedule patients. You can pre-schedule the patient before they leave the office, send reminders, and they can call to get scheduled.

Statistically, scheduling before they leave the office is the most efficient and effective way. Ideally, we have a focus on pre-scheduling our patients before they leave the office for their re-care and treatment appointments. Most dental offices "feel" like they pre-schedule 98% of their patients for their next re-care appointment, but sadly, the true metric runs around 60%.

You will want to see this at 90% to 95% to have a strong re-care program. When prescheduling this many patients, you need to control your schedule to ensure that your hygiene department has time reserved to convert period, three- and four-month period maintenance, and new patients. This "supply and demand" control is very important to maintain the integrity of your patient care.

Scheduling patients using text messages, emails, and calls is another way that many dental practices choose to re-acquire those lost hygiene patients. There are a lot of software choices that send these messages out automatically and efficiently. However, these are very impersonal and do not connect with the patient in a deeply caring way. Some practices perform a follow-up phone call after these messages have been sent, and that is also a beneficial connection that leads to conversion to an appointment. The reality is that, post-covid, most dental offices are short-staffed in the front office, and the team just does not have the time to make these calls. We cross our fingers and hope that the patient will call back to get scheduled. Hope is not a great business plan!

What can we do? We can create value for our dental visits. We can share everything that we do and connect the value to the patient about that procedure. If we are performing an oral cancer screening (you should be), then talk about it! Share statistics about oral cancer and how this is the first line of defense.

We can train our patients to keep their appointments, which cuts down on no-shows and short-notice cancellations. Print out your emails and text messages, hand this to the patient when scheduling them, and ask them to make sure that this appointment is going to work for them. Ask them to be on the lookout for these reminders and to confirm their appointment. Ask them to call as soon as possible if the appointment doesn't work so that you can get them rescheduled quickly and share the opening with someone who is waiting to get in to see the doctor and hygienist.

At SupportDDS, we have trained our candidates on customer service and the importance of getting patients scheduled for their health. Our candidates can work proactively on your practice by personally calling all of your patients who are not scheduled for their appointment. They can call the patients who are overdue for their recall appointment. They can connect with human beings to show that they care.

Our team can also make calls to the patients who have had treatment diagnosed but haven't scheduled for it yet. The team is trained to ask the patient, "Is the area hurting you yet?" They are trained to be empathetic and to be problem solvers. Most dental offices have an average of $500,000 in unscheduled treatment. Imagine, all it would take is for your team member to schedule two crowns, and they have covered the cost of their monthly fee! We have had team members who have gotten more than $100,000 scheduled in one month. That is an ROI that is OFF THE CHARTS! Even if we are conservative with our conversion, they are connecting with your patients at regular intervals and reminding them of the value of their treatment. Think of it like baseball. Every call is another "at bat", and their batting average will increase incrementally.

The Bottom Line

The more proactive with your practice you are, the more consistently your schedule will be full. Your patients will feel cared for and know the value of the services that you provide.

Chapter Seven
Executive Assistants

Outsourcing Executive Assistant Role: The Benefits of Hiring a Remote EA

As businesses grow and become more complex, the role of the executive assistant (EA) becomes increasingly important. EAs play a vital role in supporting executives and managing their busy schedules, allowing them to focus on their core responsibilities. However, finding and hiring the right EA can be a challenge, especially for small and growing businesses.

This is where outsourcing the executive assistant role can provide a solution. Outsourcing an EA allows businesses to access the expertise of highly skilled professionals without the need to hire and train in-house staff. This can save time, reduce costs, and provide a flexible and scalable solution for businesses of all sizes.

Benefits of Hiring a Remote EA

Cost Savings: Hiring a remote EA can reduce the costs associated with hiring and training in-house staff as well as the overhead costs of maintaining a physical office.

Access to Specialist Expertise: Remote EAs are highly skilled and experienced professionals who can provide expert support and manage complex tasks.

Increased Productivity: By outsourcing the EA role, executives can focus on their core responsibilities and increase their productivity as their EA manages their schedule and handles administrative tasks.

Flexibility: Hiring a remote EA provides businesses with the flexibility to scale their support as their needs change without having to hire additional staff.

Improved Work-Life Balance: By outsourcing the EA role, executives can achieve a better work-life balance as they no longer need to devote time and energy to administrative tasks.

In conclusion, outsourcing the executive assistant role can provide businesses with several benefits, including cost savings, access to specialist expertise, increased productivity, flexibility, and improved work-life balance. This makes outsourcing an attractive option for businesses that want to reduce costs, improve efficiency, and support their executives and leadership teams.

Chapter Eight
Accounting Services

Outsourcing Accounting Services: The Benefits of Working with an External Provider

In today's fast-paced business environment, many companies are turning to outsource accounting services as a way to reduce costs, improve efficiency, and free up time and resources to focus on their core operations. Outsourcing accounting services involves partnering with an external provider to handle specific accounting tasks such as bookkeeping, payroll, and tax preparation.

Benefits of Outsourcing Accounting Services

Cost Savings: Outsourcing accounting services can help companies reduce their operating costs as they no longer need to hire and train in-house accounting staff.

Access to Specialist Expertise: Outsourcing accounting services allows companies to access the expertise of specialized professionals who have the skills and experience required to handle complex accounting tasks.

Improved Accuracy and Compliance: Outsourcing accounting services can help companies maintain accurate and up-to-date financial records, reducing the risk of errors and ensuring compliance with regulatory requirements.

Increased Focus on Core Operations: By outsourcing accounting services, companies can focus on their core operations and business strategy rather than having to devote time and resources to managing their financial systems.

Scalability: Outsourcing accounting services allows companies to scale their accounting systems and services quickly and easily as their needs change without having to hire additional staff.

In conclusion, outsourcing accounting services can provide companies with several benefits, including cost savings, access to specialist expertise, improved accuracy and compliance, increased focus on core operations, and scalability. This makes outsourcing an attractive option for companies that want to reduce costs, improve efficiency, and stay ahead of the financial curve.

Chapter Nine
IT Support

Outsourcing IT Services and System Design: An Overview

In recent years, outsourcing IT services and system design has become a popular trend for businesses of all sizes. This trend has been driven by the increasing complexity of technology, the need for specialized expertise, and the desire to reduce costs and improve efficiency.

Outsourcing IT services and system design involves partnering with an external provider to handle specific IT tasks and responsibilities, such as software development, network management, and data storage. This allows businesses to focus on their core competencies and operations while outsourcing the management of their IT systems to experienced and specialized professionals.

Benefits of Outsourcing IT Services and System Design

Cost Savings: Outsourcing IT services and system design can help businesses reduce their operating costs as they no longer need to hire and train in-house IT staff.

Access to Specialist Expertise: Outsourcing IT services allows businesses to access the expertise of specialized professionals who have the skills and experience required to handle complex IT tasks.

Improved Efficiency: Outsourcing IT services and system design can improve the efficiency of business operations as external providers have the resources and processes in place to deliver high-quality services quickly and effectively.

Scalability: Outsourcing IT services and system design allows businesses to scale their IT systems and services quickly and easily as their needs change without having to hire additional staff.

Increased Focus on Core Competencies: Outsourcing IT services and system design allows businesses to focus on their core competencies and operations, rather than having to devote resources to managing their IT systems.

In conclusion, outsourcing IT services and system design can provide businesses with several benefits, including cost savings, access to specialist expertise, improved efficiency, scalability, and increased focus on core competencies. This makes outsourcing an attractive option for businesses that want to reduce costs, improve efficiency, and stay ahead of the technology curve.

Chapter Ten
Software and UX Design

Outsourcing software and UI/UX design is a popular practice for businesses that want to leverage external expertise to improve their software development and design capabilities. By outsourcing these services to third-party vendors or individuals, businesses can gain access to a wide range of benefits, including cost savings, access to expertise, faster time-to-market, flexibility, and the ability to focus on their core competencies.

One of the primary benefits of outsourcing software and UI/UX design is cost savings. By outsourcing these services, businesses can eliminate the need for additional office space, equipment, and employee benefits that would be required if they were to hire and maintain an in-house team. This can significantly reduce overhead costs and help businesses operate more efficiently.

In addition to cost savings, outsourcing software and UI/UX design can also provide businesses with access to specialized expertise. Third-party vendors and individuals often have a wealth of experience and knowledge in software development and design, which can help businesses stay up to date with the latest industry trends and technologies. This can be especially valuable for businesses that don't have the resources to invest in ongoing training and development for their in-house teams.

Outsourcing software and UI/UX design can also help businesses accelerate their development and launch timelines. By leveraging the expertise of specialized teams, businesses can often complete projects more quickly and efficiently than they would be able to with an in-house team. This can be especially important for businesses that operate in fast-paced industries where time-to-market is a critical factor.

Another benefit of outsourcing software and UI/UX design is flexibility. Outsourcing provides businesses with the flexibility to scale their operations up or down as needed without the constraints of hiring and firing employees. This can be especially valuable for businesses that experience fluctuations in demand, or that need to quickly ramp up their operations to meet a sudden surge in demand.

Finally, outsourcing software and UI/UX design can help businesses focus on their core competencies. By outsourcing these services to external vendors or individuals, businesses can free up their in-house teams to focus on the tasks and projects that are most important to their core business. This can help businesses operate more efficiently and effectively and ultimately drive better business outcomes.

In conclusion, outsourcing software and UI/UX design can provide businesses with a range of benefits, including cost savings, access to expertise, faster time-to-market, flexibility, and the ability to focus on their core competencies. While there are some potential drawbacks to outsourcing, such as a lack of control over the development process and potential communication issues with external vendors, the benefits can often outweigh the risks for businesses that are looking to improve their software development and design capabilities.

Chapter Eleven
Spanish Speakers

Why Outsource from Costa Rica: A Growing Trend in the Global Business Landscape

In recent years, Costa Rica has been gaining popularity as a hub for outsourcing services, particularly in the areas of customer service, software development, and other business support functions. It stakes its future on the potential of its people, its commitment to sustainability, and its use of technology. Over the years, Costa Rica has developed a vibrant and highly educated workforce along with a culture that embraces innovation and technology.

Benefits of Outsourcing from Costa Rica

One of the main reasons for this growth is the highly educated population of Costa Rica. The country places a strong emphasis on education, with a large percentage of its population holding university degrees. Businesses have access to a talented pool of individuals who are capable of handling complex tasks and providing high-quality services. This educated population has resulted in a more dynamic and productive economy with a strong focus on technology, innovation, and globalization.

Another factor that makes Costa Rica a desirable outsourcing destination is its close cultural proximity to the United States. This has made it easier for US-based businesses to work with providers in Costa Rica, as they share many of the same values and work ethics. This cultural familiarity has also made it easier for employees in Costa Rica to understand and meet the needs of their US-based clients. The population of Costa Rica is well-educated, with a literacy rate of nearly 95%

English also plays an important role in the education system of Costa Rica, which has helped the country develop a strong proficiency in the language. Costa Rica consistently ranks first on the TOEIC and TOEFL IBT exams, indicating a high level of English proficiency among its citizens. This is important for businesses that require their outsourcing partners to communicate effectively in English.

In conclusion, outsourcing to Costa Rica is becoming a popular trend in the global business landscape due to the country's highly educated citizens, cultural proximity to the United States, and strong proficiency in English.

As the outsourcing industry continues to grow, Costa Rica is likely to play an increasingly important role in providing businesses with high-quality services and support. The country has also made great strides in improving its economy and infrastructure, which can only further increase its attractiveness as an outsourcing destination.

Chapter Twelve

Getting the Most Out of Your Insourced Employee

What Must You Do?

We provide courses to prepare your new employee for specific functions they will be performing for you. However, it is important to note up front that the future success of your new employee will rise and fall according to the training you give them.

Of course, the amount of training varies according to each job position, but if you commit to allowing someone on your team to provide continuous direction and instruction to your new employee over the first several weeks, you will see amazing results. Your new employee will acclimate to the team quicker, have more confidence, and learn new things faster. This always leads to long-term success.

Also, it is proven that crucial to morale, stress level, and personal health is the ability to take time off from your job. We realize this, so we allow your employee one day of paid time off every month they work. You are responsible for this accrued leave, just like any of your other employees, which is part of your flat rate fee. We also ask you to give them the same holidays as your company is taking now. Typically, these include Easter/Good Friday, Memorial Day, July 4th, Labor Day, one or two days for Thanksgiving, and one or two days at Christmas. The holiday schedule should follow the same as offered in your company policy.

What Will We Do?

We provide systems to help monitor your employees. Each person clocks in and out on a biometric system. This information is available to any client who requests a copy. Another means of monitoring is through Time Doctor. For a small fee, you can have a monthly, daily, hourly, or even real-time report of your employee's work. This report will show things such as what your employee did that day, how much time they spent on different projects, which websites they had open, and what programs were used (Excel, Word, Adobe, etc.).

The most important thing we provide for you is an Account Resource Manager (A.R.M.). This is the "go-to" person for you and your employee. This person is assigned to no more than 25 team members and will assist you in managing and caring for your team. If your employee is having a problem with any aspect of their work, your A.R.M. will assist you in getting the problem resolved quickly and efficiently. You can also use your A.R.M. to check in on your employee if you sense something might be amiss. The A.R.M. will then give you vital feedback to help keep them on track.

What If an Employee Doesn't Work Out?

We have had a few occasions when the client and the employee relationship do not align. The client might not have liked the quality of work produced or how they communicated with their customers, or the employee simply didn't fit the client's office culture. While that has rarely occurred, our process of moving on is quick and straightforward. We handle the release of your current employee, which is much less painful for you than doing it in person. (If you are like me, that is the hardest [and worst] part of being a business owner.) Our Human Resources department then begins immediately interviewing other candidates to find you a new employee. Within one to two weeks, you will be up and running again. Think of how much easier that is than starting all over from square one and doing it all yourself.

The Takeaway

Training, accountability, on-site assistance through your A.R.M. and paid time off are just a few of the many things that will make your new employee successful. During your time together with your employee, we will make every effort to assist you in making the relationship successful. Also, in the rare case it doesn't work out, we handle that for you.

Chapter Thirteen

How Much Can I Save?

The Real Numbers.

When all factors, such as salary, payroll taxes, social security payment, office space, and insurance, are taken into consideration, you can expect to save from 65% to 75% annually. Let's take a look.

A $75,000-a-year employee in the United States will come in at around $100,000 a year in total costs when you factor in benefits such as vacation, health insurance, workman's compensation, payroll taxes, and FICA. These are hard numbers, not estimates. With us, that same $100,000-a-year position will typically fall within the $20,000 to $24,000 range. That is quite a savings!

One of our premier clients is London based and provides payroll services. They require high-end auditors to process payroll, audit the previous month's billing, ensure employees are paid, and match billing hours to the customers. Now they pay $20,000 to $27,000 a year for their team of fourteen to have the same tasks accomplished, saving them over 65%.

The highest savings we've provided was to a large Dental Service Organization. They required a financial analyst who was to review over twenty dental practices. His responsibility was financial analysis and ensuring that all the general ledger accounts matched up across all the spectrums. This meant bringing together hundreds of individual categories across those twenty businesses, both individual and consolidated. The C.F.O. of the organization informed us that this position was a $160,000 to $180,000 per year position with benefits. We were able to fill it for $55,000. That's over $100,000 in savings! This was the position previously not considered by the client because it didn't fit into their budget. Now, with such a reduced cost, they were able to hire this analyst and, in turn, provide more time for the C.F.O. to focus on his work.

Another one of our clients is a small I.T. company. They had numerous opportunities in their industry, but they needed a full-time help desk staffed with I.T.-type personnel to cover the hours of 6:00 am to 10:00 pm. Through us, they were able to institute a help desk program that would have cost them $140,000 to $160,000 a year for only $50,000 per year for two team members. These savings are often mind-boggling for our clients.

Even More Examples

Let me run through a few more examples of the cost savings our clients are currently enjoying.

One of our clients has an accounting manager who handles their books, prepares quarterly estimates and taxes, and manages the payroll. This was an $80,000-a-year position, for which they are now paying $28,000 annually.

An animation company has two 3D animators for whom they pay $28,000 apiece. In the United States, those same animators would run $75,000 to $90,000.

For admin support, a competent person with a quality education will run you $50,000 to $60,000 annually (including hard costs and benefits). We provide well-educated, experienced team members to do the same job at $19,000 to $22,000.

For a full-stack developer, we have clients paying $32,000 for people who command $90,000 to $120,000 in the United States.

By now, you probably get the picture. We can save you substantial amounts of money. Whether you're an independently owned mom-and-pop business, a new start-up, or a well-established company (some of our clients

eclipse $100 million in annual revenue), we can
help grow your business for less.

Key Takeaway

In starting, growing, or taking over a business,
the task of adding new employees can be
staggering. To help you with this, we can save
you 50% to 75% in salary costs. Pretty good,
huh?

Chapter Fourteen
The 51

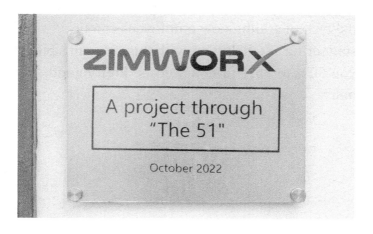

My partner and I are active Christians who are kingdom-minded. We created this business to put people back to work who were well-skilled and wanted to provide for their families. As we formulated a plan, we decided that this organization could also be a ministry for us to make a positive impact in the world. At that point, we decided to give 51% of all profits to Christian ministries. We even signed an agreement stating such. Now, God is using us to make a global impact around the world.

Win, Win, Win

I like to think about our business as a Win, Win, Win.

First, it's a Win for you as a business. We provide employees to you with substantial savings so you can grow your business.

Second, it's a Win for the people of Zimbabwe. As mentioned earlier, Zimbabwe is in an unemployment crisis. In such economic environments, one person having a job means the ability to feed a family of four or six or even an extended family. Providing this opportunity brings joy to our clients. They ask us all the time: "Hey, could you have somebody take a good picture of our employee? We want to put it in our office. They work for us, and they are part of the family." You can participate in life impacts like this as well.

Third, it's a win for Christian ministries around the world. Over the years, I've participated in overseas ministries. One of which is caring for Haiti's people in the aftermath of the 2011 earthquake. Since that time, I have made 20+ trips to that country. On one of those trips a few years back, I remember thinking, "You know what, I just need to sell everything, move down to Haiti, and make an impact." However, in my prayer time, I felt God telling me, "J.W., I need you to make profits in your business so I can make an even bigger impact around the world. I have plenty of people who can come down here and live, but I need someone to be a funnel to pass financial resources through."

From that point forward, that became a mission in my life. One of the many success stories I have is contributing to an orphanage in Haiti and assisting kids to go to a university or technical school after leaving the orphanage. One of the children, Judnel, has grown and is now going to medical school to be a doctor back in Haiti. I know that Judnel is going to make a huge difference in his country, and I am proud to say that God used me to play a small part in that.

Some Positive Impact Stories

One of the ministries we support is Global Impact (global impact-now.com). This is a non-profit/501(c)(3) that actively invests in the people of Zimbabwe, the community, and people worldwide.

During the recent pandemic, we were able to feed 322 broken families in the community of Epworth. These families are mostly headed by single women who had been left with disabled children to care for without any government or social support programs. The children range from babies to young teens, with some reaching into their twenties. These families were out of food and in desperate need of assistance. We stepped in to make a difference.

We have a healthcare consulting firm in the USA that made a personal visit to Zimbabwe with four members from their team. My wife and I were able to show them the beauty of Africa and allow them to see their employees in action first-hand. They also visited the community of Epworth. While there, they saw the hope given to these desperate families, and it made a marked difference in all of their lives. While they had always been invested in their two employees, they came away even more committed, knowing that their money was impacting not just their employees but also people like the families of Epworth.

One of our clients has an extensive dental practice in Fort Worth, Texas. They have Melody on their team, who works for them in Harare. Every time I head to Africa, they ask me, "Hey, we want to send a care package to Melody, some goodies from our office, and handwritten notes and cards." I feel like a pack mule, but I haul it over there and deliver because doing so makes the team in Fort Worth feel happy. As for Melody? You can't imagine the smile on her face when she feels the love they send.

The value of lower-cost, well-qualified remote employees is priceless, especially in a post-pandemic market. I would prefer to have qualified remote employees dealing with the day-to-day hassles of insurance and phone communications while my in-office team delivers exceptional customer service for the patients that are face-to-face inside our office!

I will never go another day without qualified remote employees from SupportDDS!
Nikki Green, *a client of SupportDDS in Zimbabwe for 5+ years!*

The Takeaway

We often hear from business owners, "I'm serving my community, but what kind of impact am I making in the world?" In response, we tell them, "We have the perfect opportunity to do just that. Not only will you be saving money and growing your business, but you will also be helping a needy family in dire circumstances. A good portion of what you are paying to us is going to assist people worldwide. It doesn't get better than that."

This is why we do what we do. We can talk all day about *what* we do and *how* we do it, but I think the most important thing is *why* we do it. We want to bless your business, bless the men and women in Zimbabwe, and bless ministries around the world. That's why we do what we do.

Chapter Fifteen
How Do I Get Started?

Our process is quick and straightforward. There are two ways to begin. First, you can go to SupportDDS.com and click "Request a Call Back." From there, you can schedule a convenient time to set up a call. Second, you can go to SupportDDS.com and click on the button that says, "Begin Here," and fill out the job matrix. We will then contact you to review our processes and answer any questions you might have. Once either of these is complete, you can sit back and relax as we begin the short journey to find you the perfect employee.

Chapter Sixteen
About the Author

Education and Experience

I was an early entrepreneur myself. In the seventh grade, my sister used to buy me the big box size of POP ROCKS at the grocery store. If you remember, you put the rocks in your mouth, and they popped. Genius! Back then, you could buy them for five cents a pack if you purchased them in a pack of 50. My sister Jamie loaned me the money to buy them. (She was out of high school by that time.) I then sold them for 10 cents a pack. Even then, I was a dreamer of owning my own business one day.

J.W. Oliver Jr. is the Managing Partner for SupportDDS and ZimWorX, with support centers in Zimbabwe and Costa Rica.

ZimWorX employs 800 team members, targeting 1,250 by the end of 2023. He has a nine-year plan to employ 20,000 team members by December 2031.

His passion is assisting organizations in leveraging growth, increasing productivity, managing costs, and freeing up time by utilizing remote/virtual teams. He is proud to be a Christian-led entrepreneur while adopting a Win, Win, Win philosophy: Creating professional opportunities and helping businesses be their very best, all while making a Global Impact by donating 51% of profits to ministries around the globe.

As an entrepreneur since age 12, selling Pop Rocks from his middle school locker, JW has started up more than 20+ companies, including a dental imaging company, an outsourcing center in Africa, an international property management group, a collegiate summer baseball team, and even a skateboard park. He is an avid traveler who enjoys seeing the world and sees an opportunity in every obstacle.

J.W. has completed two ½ Iron Men races and twelve Half Marathons, hiked six days from Cuzco to Machu Picchu, and trekked to Everest Base Camp, all after the age of 48. He is a private pilot, an ordained minister, an author, and a podcast host, and he loves to sing. He works hard to see others laugh and smile, and he desires, most of all, to uplift and encourage all he encounters to show them the love of Jesus. He has an amazing wife of almost 30 years and two awesome adult children.

Chapter Seventeen
Additional Success Stories

We have so many success stories to share. Here are just a few.

One of our clients had an existing dental office and wanted to open a second office. As a foreign dentist, she also had a language barrier to compensate for. She needed someone to be on the phone who sounded more like a person from the United States.

We managed to find her a person to handle all her insurance verifications as well as schedule appointments and make general screening calls. This dentist has now been able to open her new dental practice and enjoy substantial savings.

I manage an imaging company, am the managing partner at ZimWorX, run our non-profit Global Impact Ministry, and help my daughter with her new start-up business. In other words, I had way too many irons in the fire, and I needed help.

Then Clara arrived. Clara is exceptionally bright, motivated, and passionate about her work. As I watched her complete her tasks, I decided to elevate Clara to a higher position as my Executive Personal Assistant. She's been with me for two-and-a-half years and has taken 50% of what I do off my plate and saved me 50% in costs. She is awesome!

There was an executive who wanted to get into the animation production business. He had been dreaming of this business for 10+ years. Still, he couldn't put it into action because of the cost of animators in the United States. He just didn't have the budget.

One morning, we were having coffee, and I shared with him what we offered. In under a month, he had hired three animators in Zimbabwe and was off and running.

One of our entrepreneurs had an existing business and also wanted to start a Security Company.

However, he couldn't figure out how to do it. We helped him find the needed salespeople to go through his client list, do outbound sales calls, and talk about what they offered. Now his business is off the ground and doing well.

We also assist large companies. One of our clients is a significant medical billing company with over 500 employees. When they heard of our services, they hired five people over a span of four months and have now expanded their operations into some areas they hadn't been in before.

Made in the USA
Middletown, DE
02 September 2024